D0559478

GIN

A SHORT HISTORY

MOSES JENKINS

SHIRE PUBLICATIONS

Bloomsbury Publishing Plc

PO Box 883, Oxford, OX1 9PL, UK

1385 Broadway, 5th Floor, New York, NY 10018, USA

E-mail: shire@bloomsbury.com

www.shirebooks.co.uk

SHIRE is a trademark of Osprey Publishing Ltd

First published in Great Britain in 2019

A catalogue record for this book is available from the British Library.

ISBN:HB 978 1 78442 343 8; eBook 978 1 78442 342 1; ePDF 978 1 78442 341 4; XML 978 1 78442 344 5

19 20 21 22 23   10 9 8 7 6 5 4 3 2 1

Originated by PDQ Digital Media Solutions, Bungay, UK

Printed and bound in China by C&C Offset Printing Co Ltd

Shire Publications supports the Woodland Trust, the UK's leading woodland conservation charity.

COVER IMAGE A restorative and refreshing glass of Jinzu Gin with Luscombe Tonic Water. Gin has come a long way from its disreputable eighteenth-century image and is among the most popular drinks today. (Photograph by kind permission of Helena Bradbury: helenabradbury.com)

CONTENTS

INTRODUCTION

Gin is, at its simplest, a neutral spirit imparted with flavour from a range of plant-based materials referred to as botanicals, one of which must be juniper. If this was all there was to it, then gin would be just another one of many alcoholic spirits. The story of gin is, however, far more intriguing: it has undergone many changes in status and fortune in over 300 years since it was first drunk in Britain. The twists and turns of this intriguing history, as much as the botanicals used in its production, give gin the depth of flavour that have made it in recent decades a vastly popular drink once again. This book provides a short history of gin production and consumption in Britain and beyond.

The origins of gin can be traced to the use of juniper as a medicinal plant in the ancient world and in the use of alcoholic tonics in later centuries; when these were combined the ancestors of gin were created. Consumption of juniper-flavoured spirits for recreation was first seen in the Netherlands and Belgium where the spirit still known today as jenever is manufactured.

Today cocktails use a wide range of innovative ingredients; in this case a cocktail has been made from gin and kombucha, a type of fermented tea drink, and garnished with cucumber and rose. (Getty Images)

When gin consumption increased dramatically in Britain in the first half of the eighteenth century a moral panic was created. The spirit was blamed for all of society's ills and it took almost fifty years to curb consumption. So strong is its association with degenerate behaviour that gin has provided the English language with several phrases from that era, such as 'gin-soaked', 'gin joint' and 'gin mill', none of which have particularly positive connotations.

However, new technology in the nineteenth century enabled gin producers to improve the quality of gin on an industrial scale, leading to the development of London Dry gin. American influences led to the use of gin in cocktails so that by the 1920s it had entered a golden age of consumption and popularity.

Tastes would change in the decades after the Second World War and gin was in the doldrums for some time. The last twenty years, however, have seen the spirit soar in popularity once again. Craft producers and large distillers alike are today making gins of a quality and diversity never seen before.

From medicinal tonic to imported luxury, corrupter of the young to the basis for stylish cocktails and today a crafted product of distinction, gin is the most intriguing, versatile and adaptable spirit that can be found.

AVIATION

INGREDIENTS
60ml gin

15ml maraschino liqueur

7.5ml crème de violette

25ml lemon juice

METHOD
Add ingredients to a shaker
with ice. Shake then strain
into a cocktail glass. Garnish
with a brandied cherry.

GIN PRODUCTION

The manufacture of gin involves taking a base spirit and flavouring it with extracts from organic material known as botanicals. This chapter provides a summary of how this process is carried out, and explores some of the intriguing stories behind it.

DISTILLATION AND BASE SPIRITS

Gin starts life as a neutral alcoholic base spirit, formed by distilling a source of ethanol. In gin production this base spirit is normally formed from a fermented wash of grain. This wash is then heated in a still with vapour rising into a condenser. This process separates heavy alcohols, many of which are not wanted in modern spirit production (methanol, for example), from the alcohol that is required – ethanol. This is then commonly boiled again in a re-distillation process that separates the ethanol from water and gives a neutral spirit. To legally manufacture a distilled gin or London Dry gin within the EU the base spirit needs to have been distilled to over 96% ABV (alcohol by volume).

A pot still used in the manufacturing of gin. Although this is an older type of still than the continuous still, it is widely used today, particularly in craft gin manufacturing. (Getty Images)

Gin production on an industrial scale. This is the Goswell Road Still Room, home of Gordon's Gin in the 1950s. (Diageo)

The range of base spirits used in gin production today in many cases involve considerable innovation, although maize and barley remain the most common origin for base spirits. For example, Haymans of London use 100% English wheat to produce their base spirit. At St George Spirits in California, pot distilled rye is used as the base spirit. The Oxford Artisan Distillery uses ancient species of grain to produce base spirit working with an archeobotanist as part of the process. Some gin producers take what is sometimes referred to as the 'grain to glass' or 'field to bottle' approach, which sees them manufacture both base spirit and gin. The above-mentioned Oxford Artisanal Distillery, Copper Rivet Distillery and Chase Gin are all examples of this. Many gin makers, however, buy distilled base spirit from a distiller and then use this as the basis for making their gin.

Having either purchased or manufactured a base spirit the gin maker must then impart flavour to that spirit to transform it into gin. This flavour comes from the use of botanicals and is transferred by either distilling or compounding. There is incredible variation in the plants, seeds, fruits, spices and other organic material used in this process but essential to all gin production is juniper.

To transfer the flavour from the botanicals, the base spirit is first put into a still. In the production of some gins the botanicals are placed into the spirit itself. The spirit containing the botanicals is heated to draw out the oils and flavours of the botanicals. In others the alcoholic vapours pass through the botanicals and the flavour is transferred that way.

The earliest form of still was the pot still. In a pot still the base spirit is heated directly; alcoholic vapours then condense in a second cylindrical still by running through pipes surrounded by cold water. When producing gin in a pot still the botanicals are contained in the pot with the spirit. The first portion of spirits to come from a distillation are generally discarded as these contain impurities and would contaminate the taste of the final gin. Likewise, the end of the distillation will also be discarded. These are known as the 'heads' and 'tails' respectively.

The distillery at St George Spirits, USA. The gin produced here invokes flavours from the local area including Douglas fir, bay laurel, sage and other forest plants. (St George)

A significant development in spirit production came in 1831 when the Coffey Continuous Still was patented. It uses two columns, one filled with horizontal perforated plates that allow vapours to pass through and condense. Each plate essentially performs a distillation; the more plates there are, the purer the base spirit produced. After the heated base spirit passes through the first column it condenses in the second.

This allowed the production of a very pure spirit with a far higher degree of purity than the spirits produced in earlier distilling apparatus. A purer base spirit meant that there was much less of a need to flavour and sweeten the spirit, allowing it to be sold in a purer form. This in time came to be referred to as dry gin, giving rise to the world-famous London Dry style of gin.

A Carter Head still, also invented in the nineteenth century, is similar to a Coffey Still but sees botanicals used in a different way. In a Carter Head Still botanicals are suspended near the top of the still to allow vapour from the heated base spirit to pass through them. This is sometimes referred to as the 'gin head' method.

Whatever still is used, most distillers create a concentrated version of their gin which is then diluted with water to the

The Distillery of the New York Distilling Company, which maintains a tradition of distilling in Brooklyn dating back to the eighteenth century. (New York Distilling Company)

GIN TWIST

INGREDIENTS
45ml gin

22.5ml lemon juice

15ml sugar syrup

Boiling water

METHOD
Pour ingredients into a warmed glass and stir well. Garnish with lemon zest.

required strength, thus increasing the amount of drinkable spirit which can be produced with each distillation, although a few modern producers distil to the exact strength required to bottle. The water used for bringing gin to a drinkable strength needs to be of a high degree of purity. In the eighteenth and nineteenth centuries this saw gin distilleries cluster in certain areas, particularly in London where fresh water was at a premium. This explains the concentration of activity in gin making (as well as brewing) around the Clerkenwell district where fresh water was available.

GIN STYLES

Throughout the history of gin production a range of different styles of the drink have emerged. These are influenced by the base spirit, the botanicals used in flavouring and the methods used in manufacturing. Indeed, defining exactly what gin is can be rather problematic as there are many variations on the theme. In order to be legally classed as gin a spirit must be at least 37.5% alcohol ABV and juniper should be the dominant flavour. Within this broad definition, however, are included a wide range of drinks, all with a distinct character.

The ancestor of gin in Britain as it is consumed today is jenever. It is also known as 'genever' or 'geneva' (the name derived from the Dutch word for juniper, not from the Swiss city), or 'Hollands'. Jenever is generally produced from a fermented mash of rye or barley, which is distilled to produce

Copper is used in the making of stills of all types. This is because it is a good conductor of heat and does not allow harmful chemicals to infiltrate the spirit. (Getty Images)

PLYMOUTH GIN

TRADE MARK

IN 1620 THE MAYFLOWER SET
SAIL FROM PLYMOUTH ON
A JOURNEY OF HOPE
AND DISCOVERY

malt wine and then re-distilled to produce a juniper-flavoured spirit known as jenever. This is very different in character from what today would be considered a London Dry gin. A significant amount of flavour is retained from the rye, maize or barley, producing a depth of flavour in the base spirit that is absent from other gin types. Produced from at least as early as the sixteenth century, jenever is still drunk extensively in the Netherlands and Belgium to this day.

When gin began to be produced in Britain in the late seventeenth and eighteenth centuries (as discussed further in later chapters) the base spirit was often of dubious quality due to poor knowledge of the distilling process and the use of rough pot stills that could not produce a clean base spirit. This resulted in the addition of large amounts of additives to sweeten the spirit; botanicals such as liquorice or strong flavourings such as lemon and aniseed produced a spirit with a distinctly sugary, sweet character. This type of sweetened gin came to be known in the eighteenth century as Old Tom. The name is reported to come from a distributor of illicit gin in the period following the 1736 Gin Act, which severely restricted gin distribution. According to one legend, Captain Bradstreet established a shop with a sign in the shape of an old tomcat outside. Those seeking refreshment would place a coin in a slot underneath the cat's paw and whisper 'Puss' before receiving their beverage into a waiting jug or bottle. Another legend includes a tomcat falling into a vat of gin, but perhaps

The eighteenth century saw the production of Navy Strength gin, so called as it had to meet the Navy's proof test of soaking gunpowder in gin. (WestportWiki)

the most likely story is that it comes from the name of an early gin distiller, Thomas Chamberlain. Whatever the explanation, Old Tom became synonymous with a sweetened style of gin popular in the eighteenth and nineteenth centuries.

A further variation of gin is a high-strength type known as Navy Strength gin. In the eighteenth century the Royal Navy specified that all their ships must have a certain quantity of gin aboard. However, it was suspected that some gin being supplied to the Navy was sub-standard and diluted, as it certainly was when served to land based customers. Therefore only gin which met the standard of 100 proof (57% ABV by today's standards) was classified as 'Navy Strength'. The test for this was fairly rudimentary: a sample of gin was mixed with gunpowder, and if the gunpowder would still light it had passed the Navy's proof test. The importance of this test, as well as ensuring the Navy was not being supplied with sub-standard products, was to ensure that if a barrel of gin leaked onto a barrel of gunpowder the powder would still light.

This is likely to have been gleaned from Dutch practices. The Dutch Navy in the eighteenth century shipped jenever with a quantity of herbs referred to as 'scurvy grass' to ward off the dreaded ship-board disease. Indeed, as will be seen in later chapters, several cocktails emerged from naval life; such was the relationship between gin and the Navy that several traditions grew up around the two. New ships were provided with a 'gin commissioning kit' containing glasses and two bottles of Navy Strength gin. When a ship docked in some part of the Empire the 'gin pennant' was flown, a green and white flag, which invited fellow officers in port to come and enjoy a drink.

The style of gin known as London Dry emerged in the nineteenth century following developments in still technology described above. The purer base spirit that it was possible to achieve with a continuous still removed the need to sweeten the spirit when imparting flavour. The resulting gin was referred to as dry and, as the centre for production was London, the gin style that would dominate production in the later nineteenth and twentieth century was the London Dry style.

In modern gin production, styles are categorised according to how the flavour from botanicals is imparted to neutral spirit. For example, the botanicals can be contained within the base spirit itself during distillation or can be suspended above allowing the distilled vapours to pass through the botanicals in a process sometimes referred to as percolation. An alternative approach is to form what is termed 'cold compounded' gin, which sees oils and flavouring extracts from botanicals added to base spirit cold. London Dry gin must have all the flavour added during distillation, none is added afterwards. Dry gin also requires a very low sugar content.

Opposite
Botanicals waiting
for use in gin
distilling. The
range of botanicals
used today is truly
incredible, sourced
from across the
globe. (Diageo)

BOTANICALS

Botanicals are key to the flavouring of gin; without them the base spirit would remain flavourless, lacking taste or character. The range of botanicals used both historically and during today's proliferation of craft distilling is incredibly wide and diverse. As well as the ubiquitous juniper, spices, herbs, fruits, native wild plants and seaweeds have all been used to impart a depth of flavour.

The juniper berries used in flavouring gin can be sourced from various countries: Italy, Serbia and Macedonia in Europe, India and further afield in some cases. The berries of the juniper plant are picked in late autumn and winter and can be stored for several years to allow the oils to concentrate.

Juniper is the key
botanical in any
gin; without this
ingredient a spirit
is simply not gin.
The juniper used in
British gins today
comes mainly
from Europe.
(MPF/Wikimedia
Commons/CC 2.5)

Other botanicals are not ubiquitous but nevertheless are found in the list of ingredients of many gins: coriander seeds from Eastern Europe and Asia add a hint of spice; angelica root from the heart of central Europe provides a further taste of the forest; citrus peel from the Iberian Peninsula gives an enlivening freshness. The list of common botanicals is a long one indeed. Cinnamon and the closely related East Asian cassia add further spicy exotic notes; cardamom from the Indian subcontinent and nutmeg from Indonesia add complexity to the flavour.

Opposite: Botanicals today include material from around the world and locally sourced or foraged botanicals, creating a diverse range of flavours. (Getty Images)

The range of botanicals used today includes some very interesting ingredients. One Scottish gin uses sugar kelp as a botanical to impart local flavour and character. (Getty Images)

The three principal botanicals in a dry gin are juniper, coriander and angelica. Juniper gives gin a dry or unsweetened character. Adding anything that imparts sugariness tends to move the gin towards a sweeter style. Angelica is primarily used as a fixative for the flavours of the juniper, coriander and other botanicals. Other ingredients to fulfil the same purpose include orris root (the bulb of the iris plant). Coriander seeds give warmth to the gin and enhance citrus flavours.

To these classical botanicals can be added literally hundreds of others to create unique spirits. These are discussed more fully in the final chapter of this book and include ingredients as diverse as sea pink flowers, rowan berries, sugar kelp seaweed, tea, hibiscus and frankincense.

Coriander is one of the key botanicals, and is imported from Eastern Europe, Russia, India or North Africa. (Getty Images)

EARLY HISTORY
OF GIN

MEDICINAL ORIGINS

Given the fact that gin consumption would induce considerable moral panic in the eighteenth and nineteenth centuries, it is perhaps something of a surprise that the earliest origins of gin are, in fact, medicinal. Juniper has a long history of use as a medicinal plant: polymaths of Ancient Greece such as Aristotle extolled the health-giving properties of juniper; to the ancient Egyptians, juniper helped cure headaches; and in the ancient Arab world the plant was a curative for toothache. In medieval Europe it was believed that juniper could ward off a number of illnesses, most famously bubonic plague. The plant was burned to ward off the miasmas that were blamed for spreading the disease, and plague doctors filled their strange bird-beaked masks with herbs including juniper in an attempt to ward off infection. One physician writing in 1652 noted that juniper was useful in the treatment of stomach, eye and respiratory problems as well as aiding the memory and easing labour pains. The medicinal benefits of juniper were

The roots of early distilling lay in the work of alchemists. Searching for the elixir of life they created a drink referred to as *aqua vitae*, the water of life. (Getty Images)

appreciated well into the eighteenth and nineteenth centuries. Indeed, today juniper is still recommended for use in the treatment of stomach and kidney complaints in homeopathic medicine.

Opposite: A significant amount of early work in distilling took place in the Arab world. (Getty Images)

Of course juniper only imparts flavour to gin. A neutral alcohol spirit is also required and this, too, has its origins in the distant past of medical history. It is thought that Arabian alchemists searching for the elixir of life were the first to perform distillation resulting in the production of spirit alcohol. Much work was performed from the first century CE onwards, both across Europe and the Arab world, in developing distillation as part of alchemical work. This early work spread in the Middle Ages to European monasteries where spirit alcohol became used for restorative purposes and was known as *aqua vitae*, literally the water of life.

The combination of medicinal herbs and plants with alcoholic spirits was an obvious logical step in early medicine. As this was the first use of an alcoholic spirit flavoured with juniper here can be found the earliest iteration of the gin we drink today. Although there is no way to say exactly when the medicinal properties of

DOG'S NOSE

INGREDIENTS
330ml porter

60ml gin

3 tsp brown sugar

Nutmeg

METHOD
Add porter, gin and sugar to a pan, then grate nutmeg to taste. Gently heat until steaming hot. Serve in a heatproof glass.

The bubonic plague was one of the many diseases that juniper was credited with preventing. (Getty Images)

The earliest form of juniper-flavoured spirit used as a recreational drink was jenever, produced in Belgium and the Netherlands using stills of the kind shown here. (Getty Images)

juniper and the restorative properties of alcoholic spirit were first combined, it is likely to have been at a European monastery during the Middle Ages. One of the earliest written references to this can be found in an eleventh-century work, *Compendium Salernita*, which describes a tonic flavoured with juniper. References to juniper-based tonics appear in a number of medieval medicinal books. The first reference to a juniper-based medicinal tonic in Dutch is widely regarded as dating to 1269 in the work of Jacob van Maerlant. This is significant as it was in the Netherlands that jenever would be produced.

As early as the sixteenth century distilleries in Britain were producing 'strong water' or *aqua vitae*, sometimes flavoured with juniper. By 1600 there were at least two hundred premises distilling some form of alcoholic spirit in Britain, perhaps considerably more. Such was the production and consumption of spirits in Britain that a tax was levied on them for the first time in 1643.

Juniper-based tonics continued to be used throughout Europe into the seventeenth century. John French, an English chemist, notes in a medical text of 1653 a tonic for kidney stones, which uses juniper berries and Venice turpentine,

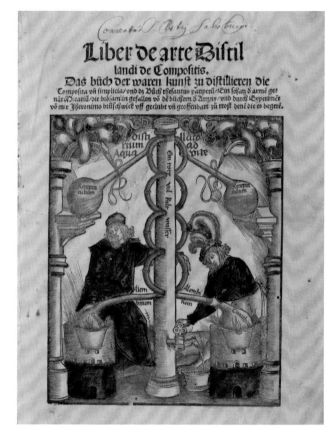

A number of books appeared in the early modern period illustrating distilling techniques. Although on a different scale, the stills used by these alchemists are not dissimilar to those used today. (Science History Institute/Public Domain)

among other ingredients. Samuel Pepys records in his diaries that he took 'strong water made of juniper' when afflicted with kidney stones. It was also noted as helping cure bladder, kidney and stomach complaints.

These developments in the production of alcoholic spirit for restorative purposes and in the use of juniper for medicinal benefits laid the foundations for the production of gin in Britain. The leap from medicinal tonic to recreational beverage would come via the Netherlands and Belgium.

EARLY JENEVER PRODUCTION

Gin can, in many ways, rightly be regarded as a native spirit to Belgium and the Netherlands, although jenever is very different in both taste and feel from the drink known today as gin.

A version of this early distilled spirit was formed from fermented grapes, referred to as 'burning wine' producing the spirit known today as brandy. A recipe from the mid-fifteenth century calls for a distillation of burned wine distilled with botanicals including juniper. Distillation from a mash of grain is believed to have been practised in the sixteenth century. This provided a neutral spirit that would form the basis of the forerunner of gin.

A drink resembling what was later known as jenever is referred to in a distilling book of 1552, the *Constelijck Distiller Book*. The man most commonly credited with inventing jenever and, by extension, gin in its many modern iterations is

Schiedam in the Netherlands has long been a centre of jenever production and today is home to the National Jenever Museum. Many jenever producers are still based here, including Nolet, Onder De Boompjes and De Kuyper. (Getty Images)

Opposite:
'Oude' (meaning 'old' in Dutch) in this jenever advertisement refers to the use of older methods of production, meaning the resulting spirit in modern terms must contain at least 15% malt wine and a given quantity of sugar - no more than 20g per litre. (Getty Images)

Sylvius de Bouvre, a scholar and alchemist from sixteenth century Netherlands. By adding juniper oil to neutral grain spirit, a tonic was created designed to treat various medical complaints. As demonstrated above, however, there were plenty of spirits flavoured with juniper around many years before Bouvre was producing his. While the precise date at which jenever came into production cannot be pinpointed, what can be said with certainty is that throughout the sixteenth century jenever was being produced in the Low Countries.

The year 1575 marks a significant watershed in the history of gin. In this year the Bulsius family established a distillery in Amsterdam. Shortening their name to Bols, these distillers of jenever are today the oldest distilling company in the world. Bols quickly established a relationship with the Dutch East India Company, which allowed them access to exotic spices and herbs for flavouring their product, and negotiated a contract to supply the company's ships with jenever, which was carried throughout the world by Dutch sailors. Bols holds particular significance in the history of gin as it was the first large-scale commercial producer of juniper-flavoured spirit for recreational rather than medicinal purposes.

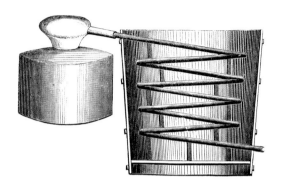

Simple pot stills such as this one would have been used in early distilling for both the production of medicinal tonics and base spirit for early alcoholic drinks such as jenever. Many craft gin producers today use similar technology. (Getty Images)

While the focus of this short history is on gin as it came to be produced in Britain and its subsequent spread throughout the world, it is important to note that jenever was never subsumed or replaced by gin. Jenever production and consumption continued in the Low Countries and is, indeed, still thriving today. Just as gin and tonic would become synonymous with the British Empire, jenever also travelled across the globe, carried overseas by colonists and traders from its shores of origin, as seen by the relationship between Bols and the Dutch East India Company. The national drink of both Belgium and the Netherlands, jenever is the grandfather of the gins that emerged in Britain and beyond.

Britain's association with gin would come via a new monarch and a pan-European conflict. It is likely that jenever was imbibed by British soldiers fighting in the many continental wars of the seventeenth century including the Thirty Years' War. Indeed, it is from the habit developed among soldiers of taking a measure of jenever before battle that the phrase 'Dutch courage' comes. A significant boost to the popularity of gin came with the arrival of William of Orange as monarch of Britain following the Glorious Revolution of 1688. He not only popularised all things related to his home country, but also introduced favourable trade terms for jenever as opposed to spirits produced by enemies of Britain and the Netherlands – Spain and France.

It was impossible for importations of jenever from the Netherlands to keep up with demand in Britain and entrepreneurs were soon looking to establish distilleries for producing jenever-style drinks for a home market. Only small quantities of jenever were imported into Britain in the seventeenth century. This meant, as with other imported wines and spirits, it was generally a drink of the upper classes. The gin produced in Britain, however, was very different in character and quality from that which came from overseas.

The jenever distillery of Lucas Bols was established in 1575. The company quickly established a relationship with the Dutch East India Company. (Public Domain)

MOTHER'S RUIN:
THE EIGHTEENTH CENTURY

The scene was thus set towards the end of the seventeenth century for gin production in Britain. A nascent distilling industry had developed from the production of medicinal tonics, and imports of jenever had given Britain a taste for juniper spirits. Furthermore, several changes in British law in the late seventeenth and early eighteenth centuries enabled gin production to increase exponentially. The first of these, in 1689, was an Act of Parliament banning the importation of French spirits; a further Act of 1690 meant that only a token payment of customs duty was required before someone could commence a distilling business. This also meant farmers and landowners could use excess grain to produce cheap spirit. In 1713 an Act stated that anyone could distil spirits at home from British malt, and a fourth Act in 1720 stated that if spirits were distilled in a house, the owner would not be required to take a billeted soldier into their home – which at the time was a significant incentive. As is so often the case, however, the law of unintended consequences meant that in addition to the various individual aims of these pieces of legislation they also

A cooper at work assembling barrels at Coates Gin Distillery, Plymouth. Plymouth gin is the basis for a drink consumed by sailors known as 'mahogany', made from two parts of gin and one part warmed black treacle. (Getty Images)

ensured that production of cheap gin rocketed in the early part of the eighteenth century, and led to what became known as the 'gin craze'.

Although the exact dates vary in interpretation, the gin craze was a phenomenon of the first half of the eighteenth century, at its height between 1720 and 1750. Largely restricted to the urban poor, particularly of London, cheap gin became a way for those at the lowest echelons of society to escape the monotonous hell that was their existence in pre-industrial Britain. With the disposable income to find temporary relief but insufficient means to escape poverty in a meaningful way, solace was sought at the bottom of a gin bottle.

The quality of much of the gin produced at this time could, at best, be described as questionable. While jenever was a sophisticated beverage with much thought given to taste, the gin produced in the back alleys and slums of eighteenth-century London was nothing like its Dutch counterpart. Poor quality grain spirit was mixed with an incredibly toxic array of other materials, including turpentine and sulphuric acid. The taste was then masked by the use of further adulterates. Not all gin produced at this time was of such a toxic quality; a simple recipe for making gin was noted in *The Complete Distiller* by A. Cooper in 1757. This called for three pounds of juniper, ten gallons of proof spirit and four gallons of water to be heated by a gentle fire, the resulting gin to be made up to the required strength with clean water. This is not so far from modern-day

The dichotomy between the way in which gin drinking and consumption of other alcoholic drinks was viewed in the mid-eighteenth century is captured in this cartoon from the 1750s. The man on the right, despite being drunk on wine, is proudly proclaiming his opposition to gin drinking. (Getty Images)

ONE OF THE COMMITTEE ON DRUKENESS AND ONE OF A
DRUNKEN COMMITTEE.

FRENCH SEVENTY-FIVE

INGREDIENTS

45ml gin

20ml lemon juice

20ml sugar syrup

30ml Champagne

METHOD

Add the ingredients, except champagne, to a shaker with ice. Shake well and strain into a champagne flute. Top with the champagne. Garnish with lemon peel

gin production but a long way from spirits made using turpentine and sulphuric acid!

This spirit was most commonly consumed in establishments known as gin shops. Often little more than a single room of a house, these were places where gin was drunk quickly and the patron encouraged to depart to make space for the next customer. Alternatively customers could take their gin home in whatever container they contrived to bring.

During the mid-eighteenth century, gin (and indeed the consumption of spirits in general) came under attack from all sides: moral, religious, health and economic. Religious organisations such as the Society for Propagation of Christian Knowledge proclaimed it a Christian duty to fight gin drinking. Noted figures such as the author Henry Fielding described gin as a poison and blamed it for rising crime rates. Gin was also (in all probability rightly so at this time) blamed for a wide range of medical complaints, including

No. 20. New Series.

HER FIRST GLASS.

The ominously titled *Her First Glass*, the implication clearly being that this upstanding woman was starting off on the road to ruin through gin consumption. (Getty Images)

liver problems and jaundice, by various august groups including The Royal College of Physicians – this was the first time they had criticised alcohol consumption on public health grounds. Ironically, these medical complaints were among those that juniper tonics were credited with curing when it was taken medicinally. Particular concern was expressed about babies being born weak or deformed and suffering from what we know today as foetal alcohol syndrome. Such babies were often described as being shrivelled and looking old beyond their years.

Other economic woes laid at the door of gin included the accusation that the poorest members of society spent what little disposable income they had on the spirit. Gin was blamed for the alms houses filling up as the poor spent money on gin rather than food. Even national security was thought to be under threat from gin; who would fight in the army and man naval ships if babies were sick and deformed?

Artists began to take up the crusade against gin, with William Hogarth famously portraying *Gin Lane* as a place of debauchery and ruin in contrast to the more wholesome *Beer Street*. This image, perhaps more than all the sermons and pamphlets, focused the minds of those who wished to restrict gin sales to the masses. Authors also poured their creative talent into attacking gin consumption, such as Henry Fielding, who wrote a pamphlet examining the causes of crime in London: 'many of these wretches there are who swallow pints

Gin Lane by William Hogarth perhaps did more than any other piece of anti-gin propaganda to focus the minds of those in power to the perceived ills caused by the spirit. All of human misery and degradation is here laid at the feet of Madam Jenever. (Wellcome Collection/ CC BY 4.0)

Despite association with the gin craze and the negative effects of gin consumption, many notable brands began production in the eighteenth century. Curtis Gin is one example of this, proclaiming proudly on later advertising their eighteenth-century roots. (Getty Images)

THE GIN
without a Parallel

Those who **KNOW**...
know **Curtis Gin**
the world over

As distilled in London since 1709

THE CURTIS DISTILLERY COMPANY LIMITED, LONDON. Export Concessionaires: Crosse & Blackwell Ltd., 20 Soho Square, London, W.1.

of this poison within the twenty-four hours; the dreadful effects of which I have the misfortune every day to see, and to smell too.'

The moral panic among those in power was fed by lurid accounts of crimes committed by the seemingly uncontrollable masses fuelled by gin. Gin was implicated in a number of grizzly crimes of the period, spread through ballads and broadsheets to an insatiable audience. A common criticism of gin was that it led to promiscuity and encouraged wanton behaviours, especially among women. Stories were printed in the press and in pamphlet form of women abandoning their children and the carelessness of those intoxicated with gin causing the death and disfigurement of their children. A greater fear, perhaps, than the moral corruption of the lower orders was that if left to become uncontrolled, they might seek to change the social order.

Realising the problems gin was causing, the government of mid-eighteenth century Britain was compelled to act. Between 1729 and 1751 no fewer than eight Gin Acts were passed by Parliament. The day before one of these Acts was passed in 1736 crowds rioted in London. Gin shops draped their signs in black mourning cloth, ballads were sung and mock funerals for 'Madam Genever' were held. This and the other Acts did little to reduce the consumption of gin and simply drove it underground. Gin came to be sold under new names and was frequently referred to as 'Parliament Brandy' in

mockery of the institution which had tried to restrict its consumption.

In the years when attempts were made to control the consumption of gin in Britain no such attempts were made to curb the upper classes' consumption of port, wine, imported jenever or brandy, nor, indeed, of the consumption of beer by all classes. There was a distinct dichotomy between the ways in which gin and jenever were portrayed; even as home-distilled gin was being maligned from all sides, good quality, imported jenever was still consumed by the wealthy. This is attested to by the amount of high-quality jenever that was smuggled into Britain in the eighteenth century. Indeed, one effect of the various gin Acts of the mid-eighteenth century restricting home production of gin was to increase the market for smuggled spirits. A particularly lucrative smuggling route for gin was between Rotterdam and Scotland. A Guernsey smuggler in the mid-eighteenth century was caught smuggling 'genever' among other commodities. There was also noted a thriving trade in smuggled gin and tobacco from the Netherlands into Shetland well into the nineteenth century, and between 1816 and 1823 Dutch vessels carried an estimated 10,000 gallons of illicit gin per year into Shetland.

A mock funeral for 'Madam Geneva', drawn in 1751 when the last Gin Act was passed. The mourners are the distillers of gin with those who consumed the spirit watching on. Although the 1751 Act had some success at limiting gin consumption, predictions of the death of Madam Jenever were premature.

The government finally cracked down on gin in a meaningful way in 1751, the same year *Gin Lane* was published. Gin was banned from being sold in shops, it was banned from alms houses and prisons and, perhaps most effective of all, duty on the spirit was substantially increased. Licensed premises could only sell alcohol if they paid rates of at least £10 per year, resulting in the closure of numerous gin shops. Those who hawked gin on the street faced draconian penalties, a second offence saw imprisonment and a whipping, a third offence and it was transportation to the colonies. The final Gin Act of 1751, along with various other societal factors, led to the gin craze subsiding in the mid-eighteenth century. Crop failures, a prohibition on the use of grain for distilling, and changing tastes led to a fall in gin consumption in the 1750s. In 1751 around 7 million gallons of gin was taxed; within a year this had fallen to 4.4 million and by the end of the 1760s the figure was just less than 2 million gallons.

As well as the poor-quality back street gin distilled in Britain, gin was also imported in the eighteenth century and sat alongside other foreign spirits such as brandy and port in the homes of the wealthy. (Getty Images)

RISING QUALITY:
THE NINETEENTH CENTURY

In the early nineteenth century gin-drinking patterns in Britain continued much as they were at the end of the eighteenth. Gin drinking among the working poor continued, and while the worst of the gin shops had faded from memory there were still plenty of taverns, alehouses and inns at which workers could quench their thirst with gin. The seeds of better quality production had been sown towards the end of the eighteenth century when firms such as Gordon's began producing gin, although those who could afford to continued to consume their imported jenever. The nineteenth century saw considerable changes in gin consumption and production, including the emergence of many famous names that will be familiar to gin drinkers today.

GIN AND TONIC

As with the spirit itself, the origins of the ubiquitous gin and tonic are also medicinal, developed from a need among European colonists to ward off malaria. The medicinal benefits of quinine as a protection against malaria had been recognised

Gilbey's Gin commenced operations in 1872 and later expanded to open distilleries in Australia and Canada in the twentieth century. Orange peel is one of the twelve botanicals used. (Getty Images)

Alexander Gordon, a name synonymous with gin, founded his distilling company in the eighteenth century. The boar's head crest of the family Gordon can still be found on bottles of Gordon's Gin to this day. (Diageo)

since the seventeenth century, and in 1768 a British naval doctor prescribed a measure of powdered cinchona bark, the source of quinine, for sailors when in tropical countries, although it was not widely adopted. The cinchona tree is not native to Britain but was planted around the Empire in the nineteenth century. Quinine was extracted from the bark and this was used to make a medicinal tonic. This tonic, however, had a very bitter taste and in an attempt to make the medicine more palatable it was drunk with various additives such as sugar and lime or, alternatively, was heavily watered down. Gin was a familiar drink to British colonists throughout the Empire in the nineteenth century and it took little stretch of the imagination to add the spirit to the quinine tonic. The gin and tonic was born and was brought back to Britain by those returning from India, soon becoming a recreational as opposed to a medicinal drink. An enterprising drink manufacturer, Erasmus Bond, began to produce 'tonic water' for use in gin and tonics in 1858, and in 1871 the Schweppes Company (founded by Johann Schweppe in 1783) introduced their famous India Tonic Water. Winston Churchill would encapsulate the connection between the G and T and

Bottles such as this allowed carbonated drinks to be sold for the first time, including tonic water marketed specifically for use in gin and tonics by companies such as Schweppes. (Collection of Auckland Museum/ CC by SA 4.0)

Quinine. The origin of the gin and tonic, as with the origin of gin itself, was medicinal. (Wellcome Collection/ CC BY 4.0)

the British Empire when he stated, 'The gin and tonic has saved more Englishmen's lives and minds than all the doctors in the Empire.'

THE RISE OF DRY GIN AND NEW COMPANIES

The nineteenth century saw several advances in distilling techniques. As we have seen, the most significant of these was the invention of the Coffey Still, patented in 1830. The continuous still produced a purer spirit in a more economical way than the pot still, allowing botanicals to come to the fore and removing the need for sweetening. Old Tom would quickly give way to London Dry gin.

As continuous stills allowed a greater amount of spirit to be produced, it became possible for professional distillers who had started up their businesses towards the end of the eighteenth century to expand, making gin on a scale hitherto unknown. It is at this time that recognised brands come to the fore: Alexander Gordon established his distillery at Clerkenwell in 1786; in 1830 Charles Tanqueray began distilling gin at his Bloomsbury Distillery; Beefeater was launched in 1876; and Gilbey's began production in 1872. In 1898 Tanqueray and Gordon's merged in the first coming together of major gin brands. The Gordon clan crest boar is still on the bottle to this day. These companies were all based in London, clustered around Clerkenwell due to the purity of water available.

By the end of the nineteenth century gin had largely cast off its reputation as a drink of the dissolute and the desperate. Art once again reflected reality with gin's new status reflected in sculptures by F.W. Pomeroy in the building of Booth's new distillery in 1899, a far cry from the paintings of *Gin Lane* and *The Dram Shop*. Dry gin, now of a high quality, became a respectable drink. Gin began to be enjoyed by upper-class gentlemen in clubs throughout Britain and beyond, and by respectable ladies. No longer mother's ruin, gin had entered the establishment.

Charles Tanqueray, founder of the eponymous gin company that would form one half of the Gordon Tanqueray gin dynasty. Both brands are now part of the Diageo company. (Diageo)

" *The House,*" *Goswell Rd*

The year 1850 was to be highly significant in the development of gin worldwide. It was in this year that the ban on exporting gin was lifted and British gin became available throughout the world. The spread of dry gin quickly began to influence producers around the world. Dry gin production in America began in 1868 when Fleischmann commenced operations that year. The nineteenth century saw the growth of a strong gin culture in America, including consumption of considerable amounts of jenever from the Low Countries; Bols started exporting jenever to America in 1832. British producers also began to establish distilleries overseas; to take just one example, Gilbey's established distilleries throughout the British Empire. Beginning in Canada and Australia they would go on to establish themselves in New Zealand, Uruguay, Namibia and Mozambique, among other countries.

This rising quality, however, was not always evident in gin that was exported from Britain to Africa in the nineteenth century. West Africa saw vast quantities of what was termed 'trader gin' sent from Britain to be exchanged for palm oil, an important component in various industrial processes at the time. In 1889, 1.35 million gallons were imported into Nigeria; by 1908 the West African gin trade was worth 1.2 million pounds with the vast majority going to Nigeria. The export of such trade gin was banned by treaty in 1919 due to the harmful effects of the spirit.

Until the development of the continuous still, gin had generally been sweetened, producing gins of the 'Old Tom' variety discussed earlier. Sweetening of the spirit was required to mask the noxious taste of the often toxic adulterants which were added. Even unadulterated gin was a much rougher spirit than that which would be produced in later years, due to impurities in still technology. There was also an expectation from consumers that gin would be sweetened, therefore even

Old Tom styles of gin remained in production during the nineteenth century but these were largely superseded by London Dry, especially in the later twentieth century when gin suffered a decline in popularity. (Diageo)

GIMLET

INGREDIENTS
75ml gin

15ml fresh lime juice

15ml sugar syrup

METHOD
Add ingredients to a shaker with ice
and shake well. Strain into a cocktail
glass filled with fresh ice. Garnish
with lime.

those who produced spirit of a quality that could be consumed unsweetened added sweeteners to their gin in order to give customers what they expected.

The production of a purer base spirit set gin free to allow botanicals to be used to provide flavour. Spices, florals, fruits and botanicals from around the world were available to British gin producers thanks to trade with the Empire. Unsweetened gin came to be advertised as 'dry' in the mid-nineteenth century, and as production was concentrated in London, this in time came to be referred to as London Dry gin. The new still technology also allowed for greater volumes to be produced at one time, which led to more consistent quality and, crucially, large firms were created who could build up power and influence.

GIN PALACES

The nineteenth century saw the drinking of gin leave the grog shop and become elevated to a higher status. It was at this time that 'gin palaces' began to be established. These gleaming hostelries, illuminated by innovative gas lighting and incorporating fashionable forms of decoration such as terracotta, faience and plate glass, were like nothing Britain had seen before. Long bar counters of carved mahogany, with engraved mirrors and gleaming brass fixtures and fittings completed the look and feel of the gin palace. The incorporation of gas lighting was designed to lure passers-by; Charles Dickens described

Opposite: The Gimlet cocktail is reputed to have originated in the Royal Navy, when lime juice was used to fight off scurvy. (Stephen Hopson/ www.stevehopson. com/CC-SA 2.5)

them as 'perfectly dazzling when contrasted with the darkness and the dirt we have just left'.

Despite this opulence, there was a lack of seating in these gin palaces, to encourage patrons to enter, drink and then leave. In this regard the principles of the eighteenth-century gin shop were still alive and well. No longer simply the preserve of an underclass drinking to forget the realities of existence, gin palaces were the theatres in which a new way of drinking gin would come to be enjoyed. Gin palaces were designed to compete with the emerging public houses, which were often tied to breweries springing up throughout the early nineteenth century.

In their early days there was a distinction between gin palaces and public houses. Public houses at this time tended to have small rooms, sometimes referred to as parlours, and provided accommodation for travellers. Food was also often sold at public houses with seating provided. The gin palace, beginning in London, spread throughout England in the 1830s and '40s and reached Scotland by the 1850s, some public houses being converted into gin palaces during this time. By the end of the nineteenth century, however, the true gin palace had all but disappeared, and a hybrid of the gin palace and public house was created, retaining some elements of the decorative schemes from the gin palace while including some of the amenities of the public house.

The gas lighting, decorative architectural detail and large casks of gin were features synonymous with gin palaces. All ages and classes can be seen attending the bar. (Getty Images)

A number of these lavish temples to Lady Jenever survive today. The Princess Louise in High Holborn, and Princess Victoria in Uxbridge are two fine examples in London. The gin palace was not restricted only to the nation's capital, however: many surviving examples can be found throughout Britain. The Philharmonic Dining Rooms, Liverpool and Bakers Vaults, Stockport are excellent examples in the north of England; The Barton Arms, Birmingham, the Crown Liquor Saloon in Belfast and Edinburgh's Guildford Arms are further examples outside London. Although not established as gin palaces in their own right, these examples give visitors today a feel for what the original gin palaces were like.

Opposite: A less-than-complimentary view of a gin palace. All the tropes from *Gin Lane* are here in this nineteenth-century image: fallen women, vulnerable children and sickly men. (Getty Images)

Here the style of the gin palace merges with the functional comforts of a public house. Many buildings of this age and style survive today, with a number of them still serving their original function. (Getty Images)

TEMPERANCE AND GIN

Almost at the same time as gin palaces were emerging, so too did a new movement against the consumption of the spirit, the temperance movement. Much of the rhetoric around gin in the nineteenth century had changed little from the end of the gin craze fifty years previously. The successors to Hogarth's *Gin Lane* were drawn at this time; *The Dram Shop*, an illustration by Thomas Rowlandson, was published in 1815, and George Cruickshank, most famous for illustrating Charles Dickens' works, drew *The Gin Shop* in 1829 and later a series

Opposite: Another gin palace showing the familiar decorative detailing. A moral message is conveyed against excess consumption of gin, with women and children present and the customer fishing around for his last penny. (Getty Images)

The *GIN* Shop.

Many of the same themes used in *Gin Lane* were taken on enthusiastically by those who sought to regulate alcohol consumption in the nineteenth century. Again gin is held responsible for leading the nation's men, women and children astray. (British Library/ CC0 1.0)

67

A further representation of the perceived evils of gin drinking in the nineteenth century. Again, consumption by children is portrayed showing the harmful effects to young and old alike. (Getty Images)

of drawings called 'The Bottle', all of which attempted to encapsulate the perceived wickedness of gin drinking. Temperance author and poet Thomas Hood also attacked gin: 'The dram of Satan!/The liquor of Sin!/Distill'd from the fell/Alembics of Hell'. The view of gin as being solely responsible for all Britain's ills in the nineteenth century was challenged somewhat by no less a figure than Charles Dickens himself, who noted: 'Gin-drinking is a great vice in England, but wretchedness and dirt are a greater'.

The temperance movement, which arose from concern about working-class drunkenness, began in the 1830s and had many fervent devotees. The British and Foreign Temperance Society was founded in 1836 with the aim of reducing the consumption of alcohol, especially spirits. The characters portrayed in the efforts of temperance activists to frighten people from the ills of gin were reminiscent of those conjured a century before during the gin craze. Once again it was the negative consequences for women and children that were thrust to the fore. Temperance hotels were constructed to provide people with a place of repast that was not the gin palace, and in 1855 the temperance movement attempted to have all Sunday opening of licensed premises banned – but this led to a riot in London.

The GIN-JUGGARNATH. Or, The Worship of the GREAT SPIRIT of the age.
—— It's Devotees destroy themselves —— It's progress is marked with desolation. misery, and Crime. ——

The Gin Juggarnath, by George Cruikshank. A fanciful depiction of the harm temperance campaigners felt was being caused by gin and other alcoholic drinks. (Getty Images)

Even the ministrations of the temperance movement could not keep gin down. As happened repeatedly in the history of gin consumption, new audiences were drawn to the melodrama that is the life of Madam Jenever. The poets and artists collectively referred to as the Romantics were drawn to the drink as an act of defiance. Led by Lord Byron, gin gained a cachet in literary and artistic circles; the painter George Morland enjoyed consuming Holland Gin, among other beverages.

Punch was the earliest mixed drink involving gin. Generally formed of a spirit mixed with citrus and spices it was mixed and served in communal punch bowls such as this one, from around 1770. (Hallwyl Museum/Jens Mohr/CC BY-SA 3.0)

COCKTAILS

Rising quality, production by large respectable companies and associations with Empire all ensured that gin in the second half of the nineteenth century would be enjoyed by those of all social classes in a way that had previously not been the case. At this time British gin came to replace imported jenever for the first time in the drinks cabinets and clubs of those at the very top of the social hierarchy. Central to this journey was the use of gin in cocktails and mixed drinks. Those visiting the Garrick Club in Covent Garden, for example, could enjoy a Summer Gin Punch made of lemon juice, gin and sugar.

This use of the spirit for cocktails had its origins in the punch bowl of the eighteenth century. At this time bartenders, especially in America, were mixing gin into punches and serving these by the glass. Punch is essentially formed of any spirit, mixed with sugar, water and flavourings (most commonly citrus). In British drinking culture before the nineteenth century punch had generally been based around rum. In America, however, a much greater range of spirits was used, most commonly gin. The first use of the word 'cocktail' in the English language appears in 1806 when it is defined as a 'stimulating liquor composed of spirits, sugar, water and bitters'. The link to both punch and early medicinal uses of bitters is clear. Another early mixed drink, a precursor to cocktails, is the gin twist. Formed by mixing gin, lemon juice, sugar and boiling water, this was very close to being simply a hot punch, a combination of punch and toddy.

Several nineteenth-century cocktails emerged from British naval life. The cocktail called the Gimlet was invented by a doctor of the Royal Navy to help fight off scurvy, the lime juice providing a much-needed dose of Vitamin C.

GIN PUNCH

INGREDIENTS

250g brown sugar

7 sliced lemons

750ml gin

750ml ginger wine

Pinch of cloves

I tsp cinnamon

I tsp nutmeg

Hot water

METHOD

Mix all ingredients except the hot water in a large punch bowl. Add hot water to taste and stir well. Serve in a punch bowl.

This was not the only contribution to cocktails made by the Navy, however. Angostura bitters were created in 1824 as a tonic against a bewildering range of maladies from malaria and colic to general weakness. Mixing the bitters with gin helped ease the taste of the medicine, giving rise to the quintessentially British colonial drink the pink gin, so called as gin and bitters leave a pinkish residue behind when drunk.

Cocktails became part of the theatre of American bar culture in the nineteenth century, with bartenders mixing the drinks in front of their customers. This saw its first iteration in print in 1862 with the publication of *How to Mix Drinks or the Bon Vivant's Companion* by an American barman, Jerry Thomas. In 1850 America got its first taste of British gin when the export ban was lifted. British Old Tom gin was specified by Jerry Thomas for many drinks including the Martinez, an

Opposite: A gin apple martini, formed simply of gin, dry vermouth and garnished with apple, one of many versions of the martini available today. (Getty Images)

Jerry Thomas, a bartender and saloon owner from New York, is regarded by many as the father of cocktail-mixing. (CakeandTail/ CC-by-SA 4.0)

JOHN COLLINS

INGREDIENTS

1 tsp powdered sugar

Juice of half a lemon

60ml Old Tom gin

Plain soda

METHOD
Shake or stir with ice. Serve with a slice of lemon peel.

early version of the Martini. The Martini would become one of the most iconic gin-based drinks of all time, famously described by American journalist H.L. Mencken as 'the only American invention as perfect as the sonnet'. Jenever was still popular in America at this time, however, and was used in many cocktail recipes of the day. It is likely that jenever-style gins were being produced in America from an early date. The first production of a dry style of gin in America was at Fleischmann's Distillery in Ohio and was undoubtedly a response to its use in cocktails.

The early nineteenth century saw the development of another gin-related mixed drink that is instantly recognisable today: Pimms. First created by the proprietor of Pimms Oyster Bar in London, Pimms House Cup (as it was known in the 1820s) used herbs, spices and liqueurs to flavour gin. This gave rise to a wide range of fruit cups and summer cups.

The ingredients of a John Collins cocktail were first noted in down in the 1860s – soda water, sugar, lemon, ice and of course gin. This is today known as a Tom Collins.

Although the gin and tonic is something of a purists' drink, it can sometimes be drunk in inventive ways; here summer fruits are incorporated. The G&T is consumed around the world and along with the martini encapsulates the glamour that is still attached to the spirit. (Getty Images)

RISE, FALL AND RISE AGAIN:
GIN IN MODERN TIMES

TEMPERANCE AND PROHIBITION IN AMERICA

Even as gin drinking, cocktails and drinking culture in general were burgeoning in America, a moral reaction similar to that seen in Britain in previous centuries was gaining traction. Temperance and abstinence movements had developed in the nineteenth century but it was the years immediately prior to and during the First World War that these movements gained political capital, culminating in the passing of the Eighteenth Amendment, which prohibited the sale of alcohol. Had those passing the Act studied the history of similar attempts in eighteenth-century Britain they could perhaps have foreseen the consequences. Predictably illicit alcohol production and consumption flourished as speakeasies were created with elaborate means of gaining entry, reminiscent of the Londoner placing a penny into the hands of Old Tom the cat.

Gin continued to be smuggled into America and British companies had no issue flouting the constitution. Bootleg

The martini, symbol of the cachet gained by gin in the twentieth century, remains iconic to this day. London Dry gin is the basis of the best martinis. (Getty Images)

spirits were also produced in great quantities, giving rise to the term 'bathtub gin', as this was often produced by simply mixing juniper essence with spirit in a bathtub. In a further parallel to the gin craze, unsuitable industrial spirits were used, resulting in many thousands of deaths. Prohibition ended in time for Christmas 1933, having been an almost unadulterated failure. Gin was legal again and production resumed almost instantly. Indeed, a number of British companies, including Gordon's in 1934 and Gilbey's in 1938, opened distilleries in America.

While prohibition was clearly catastrophic for legitimate American gin producers, gin drinking and cocktail culture on the other side of the Atlantic was entering a golden age.

THE GOLDEN AGE OF GIN

By the start of the twentieth century cocktail drinking was expanding throughout the globe. The route by which cocktail culture would explode onto the scene in Britain is somewhat surprising, however. One of the unintended consequences of prohibition was to force American bartenders to seek employment abroad. Many would hop across the pond, particularly to London, and brought with them the latest in cocktails, such as the Singapore Sling, invented in 1915.

Cocktails became a staple of the well-heeled who had the wealth and leisure to partake in what came to be known as the 'roaring Twenties'.

SINGAPORE SLING

INGREDIENTS

30ml gin

15ml cherry brandy

7.5ml Cointreau

7.5ml Dom Benedictine

dash Angostura bitters

10ml grenadine

15ml lime juice

120ml pineapple juice

ice cubes

METHOD
Combine ingredients in a cocktail shaker and shake. Strain into a pocogrande glass. Garnish with slice of pineapple and cherry.

Hotels in London such as the Dorchester, the Ritz and the Savoy had American-style bars serving cocktails. Harry's New York Bar in Paris was established by a Scottish bartender, Harry MacElhone, and could count Coco Chanel and Ernest Hemingway among its clientele. It was during this age more than any other, when cocktails were enjoyed by famous writers and glittering stars of stage and screen, that gin became a drink of glitz and glamour. Jazz was soon added to this intoxicating mix, as at the famous London Club Ciro's, reputedly a haunt of Edward VIII.

A slew of cocktail books were produced in the 1920s and '30s; the barman at the Savoy in London produced a book of recipes in 1930 entitled *The Savoy Cocktail Book*, and companies also got in on the act, Plymouth Gin producing a cocktail book in 1925.

It was at this time that companies such as Gordon's and Booth's marketed gin as the drink of the sophisticated, the wealthy and the literati. Earls and countesses were featured in advertisements that emphasised gin's versatility in cocktails. Some, such as Gordon's and Beefeater, produced ready-mixed cocktails for use in the home. Brands such as Pimms would at this time become associated with leisure pursuits such as tennis, an enduring link that is still going strong almost a century later.

British distillers also continued to expand into overseas markets. Tanqueray Gordon were taken over by the Distillers

Opposite: Ernest Hemingway pouring a glass of Gordon's Gin in 1948; a dry martini was reputedly his favourite cocktail. Gin's association with writers, artists and stars of stage and screen helped make it highly popular. (Getty Images)

Gin's appeal as the spirit of choice in a wide range of cocktails and mixed drinks can clearly be seen, in this artwork and on the bottle itself in this 1930s advertisement for Gordon's in America. (Diageo)

Drinks never taste thin with Gordon's Gin

Gordon's Gin has Liqueur Quality and High Proof, 94.4. That means richer flavor—velvety smoothness—drinks that never taste thin. Obey your sense of discrimination—always ask for Gordon's—you'll be amazed at the finer, richer, smoother taste of your gin drinks.

Gordon's Gin

100% NEUTRAL SPIRITS DISTILLED FROM GRAIN • 94.4 PROOF

Company in 1924 and made a move into production in the USA only a year after prohibition ended. In 1934 Gordon's opened a distillery in New Jersey, followed by Illinois in 1965 and California in 1971.

Gin continued to be a staple of Britain's colonial administration in establishments such as Raffles, home of the Singapore Sling. Lord Mountbatten may have enjoyed a London Dry gin when he stayed in the Imperial Hotel in New Delhi. Rudyard Kipling, Noel Coward and Somerset Maugham could have sipped fashionable cocktails at the Eastern and Oriental in Penang, all having been guests there in the interwar years. The British Empire ensured gin was enjoyed by the rich and famous throughout the world.

The place of gin in its golden age of the Twenties and Thirties was summed up beautifully by the playwright Noel Coward: 'For gin, in cruel Sober truth, supplies the fuel for flaming youth.' However, nothing can last for ever, and troubled times lay ahead for gin.

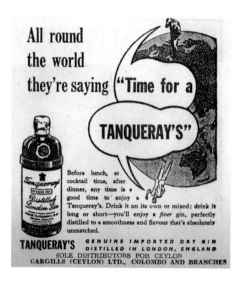

Gin continued to be associated with the British Empire and was drunk in many countries with a colonial past. This advertisement from the *Ceylon Daily News* in the 1950s shows the global appeal of London Dry gin. (Diageo)

GIN

A distinctive bottle has always been part of the marketing behind Tanqueray Gin, as shown here in this advertisement from the 1960s. (Diageo)

After the show, enjoy the limelight.

TROUBLED TIMES

The Second World War had a devastating effect on the production and consumption of gin in Britain. Many distilleries, particularly in London, were damaged or completely destroyed by bombing raids. Base spirit was requisitioned by the Army and grain was in short supply, making production difficult for those distillers that were not bomb damaged. Although most established firms would limp along through the war years, some did not re-emerge in post war Britain.

The decline suffered by gin in the decades after the end of the Second World War has been ascribed to a feeling that the drink was old-fashioned, associated with the past rather than the future, and with an Empire that no longer existed, but it was probably as much to do with simple changes in fashion and competition from other drinks. It was at this time that vodka was gaining in popularity; in the 1960s, '70s and '80s this new spirit on the block would undoubtedly have a considerable impact on gin consumption. Even James Bond was drinking vodka martini in 1962. Vodka was very much a new player in the British market although it had been popular in America for longer. Further competition came from wine drinking which gained popularity among all classes in the latter part of the twentieth century with affordable imports from around the world.

It would be wrong, however, to conclude that gin lost all of its cachet in the second half of the twentieth century.

GIN

Associations with the Empire and a particular kind of Britishness were, by the time of this 1970s advertisement, increasingly looking old-fashioned. It was hard at this time to foresee the revolution that would come in gin consumption at the end of the twentieth century. (Diageo)

Gordon's. It's how the English keep their gin up!

"By Jove, Gordon's® *is* the dry one, wouldn you say?" said the man in the bowler.

"Gin-uinely dry, my good man," answered the Cricketer.

"Matter of fact . . . every bottle of Gordon's is *still* based on that original formula!" said the Admiral.

"Of course!" replied the Barrister. "Would you re-paint a Gainsborough?"

(All of England, America, the rest of the world has agreed for over 200 years that Mr. Gordon's wonderful discovery in 1769 is responsible for more Gin-uinely delicious drinks than any other.)

Gordon's Sour
1½ oz. Gordon's Dry Gin.
Juice of ½ lemon.
½ teaspoon powdered sugar. Shake well in shaker half filled with cracked ice.
Strain into Sour glass.
Add dash of soda water.
Decorate with orange slice and cherry.

Gordon's Collins
1½ oz. Gordon's Dry Gin.
Juice of ½ lemon.
Pour into highball glass with ice cubes.
Fill with soda water.
Add a little powdered sugar.
Stir, decorate with orange slice.

Gordon's Dry Martini
4 or more parts Gordon's Dry Gin.
1 part Dry Vermouth.
Stir well in pitcher half filled with ice.
Strain into cocktail glass or serve on rocks.
Optional: add olive or twist of lemon peel.

Opposite: Gin, vermouth and a dash of bitters, all the ingredients ready for making a martini, embodiment of gin's glitz and glamour. (Achim Schleuning/ CC 4.0)

Gordon's Old Fashioned
Muddle ½ lump sugar in dash of bitters.
Add 1½ oz. Gordon's Dry Gin over ice cubes.
Add splash of soda water.
Serve in Old Fashioned glass.
Decorate with orange slice.

Gordon's & Tonic
1½ oz.
Gordon's Dry Gin.
Pour into highball glass with ice cubes and fill with tonic water.
Add slice of lemon or lime.

86

PRODUCT OF U.S.A. 100% NEUTRAL SPIRITS DISTILLED FROM GRAIN. 90 PROOF. GORDON'S DRY GIN CO., LTD., LINDEN

MARTINI

INGREDIENTS
75ml gin

15ml dry vermouth

1 dash orange bitters

Lemon twist or other garnish

METHOD
Add ingredients to a mixing glass
with ice and stir until chilled. Strain
into a chilled cocktail glass. Garnish
with lemon twist.

The appeal of gin as the basis for a martini was still a powerful advertising tool in the 1950s, even as vodka was approaching to challenge gin. (Diageo)

Beefeater exploited Elizabeth II's coronation in 1953 to drive export sales, particularly to America, while Tanqueray sought celebrity endorsement from figures such as Frank Sinatra and Sammy Davis Jr. Despite some suggestions that gin would suffer an irreversible decline, this was never the case. There is no doubt that considerable rationalisation took place in gin production in the later decades of the twentieth century. Various takeovers and mergers occurred at this time. Seager Evans was bought by an American company, the brand name of Charles Dickens' favourite gin disappearing soon after. Gilbey's left the control of its eponymous founding family for the first time in the 1960s and became part of International Distillers and Vintners which, in turn, became part of Diageo. Gin styles such as Old Tom were almost entirely discontinued during this rationalisation. Pimms continued to produce its gin-based cup but sales fell considerably.

Further rationalisation in gin production was to take place in the 1980s and into the '90s. Family connections with established gin companies were finally severed: the Burrough family of Beefeater fame sold to the brewer Whitbread in 1987, and the last member of the Tanqueray family retired from the company in the 1980s. Gin brands that had been part of the Distillers Company became part of United Distillers and, soon afterwards, Diageo. Diageo is the world's largest producer of spirits today, producing Gordon's, Gilbey's and Tanqueray, along with a wide range of other spirits.

Gin's decline in popularity during the 1980s might have been assumed to be terminal; nothing could have been further from the truth, however. This was when the seeds of a revolution in gin production and consumption were sown.

CRAFT GIN REVOLUTION

The end of the twentieth century and start of the twenty-first saw a flourishing of gin manufacturing in Britain. One could argue, however, that this craft gin revolution saw its origins in America. Small batch distilling was being carried out by companies such as St George Spirits in Alameda, California, as early as the 1980s. With their origins in the production of brandy and whisky, companies like this demonstrated the viability of craft distilling before it became a recognised phenomenon in Britain.

A giant billboard advertisement for Gordon's Gin in Time Square, New York 1971. Despite an undoubted fall in popularity in the later part of the twentieth century, gin was still consumed in large quantities and never fell completely out of favour. (Getty Images)

St George Spirits was an early example of what could be done on a craft level in gin making. Here the founder of the company, Jorg Rupf, can be seen when the company was founded in 1982. (St George)

91

The first sign something was changing in British gin production came when Bombay Sapphire gin was launched in 1987. This was the first green shoot of recovery for gin in Britain after several decades of decline. The ancestor of Bombay Sapphire lay as far back as 1761 when Warrington Dry Gin entered production. The recipe for this eighteenth-century gin was the basis for Bombay Dry Gin, which was to become Bombay Sapphire in 1987. Bombay Sapphire was conceived of as a premium brand and included innovative botanicals such as cubeb berries and grains of paradise. With a stylish bottle inspired by a sapphire and references to the former heyday of gin drinking in the Empire, Bombay Sapphire blended history with modern style and, crucially, flavour.

Early craft producers such as St George Spirits and Bombay Sapphire were certainly important trail-blazers in the revival of gin in Britain. The craft gin revolution that would occur at the start of the twenty-first century can first be seen with the launch of Hendricks gin, which began production in 1999 in Ayrshire. Although a Scottish origin for craft gin production may seem curious considering gin's undoubted association with London, it should not come as a surprise. Around 70% of British gin is produced in Scotland: Hendricks, Gordon's and Tanqueray are all produced in Scotland along with an incredible range of craft gins. Other craft producers quickly followed Hendricks onto the market;

The New York Distilling Company produces three gins, including a Navy Strength variety ('Perry's Tot') and a jenever style referred to as a 'New Netherland', once again showing how old styles are being reinvented in the craft gin revolution on both sides of the Atlantic. (NYDC)

Sipsmith began production of gin in London in 2009, the first traditional copper distillery founded in London since the early nineteenth century.

The revival in gin's fortunes has seen a number of old styles becoming popular once again. Navy Strength gin was the first of these to see a revival when Plymouth Gin, close to closure in the mid-1990s, increased the strength of its gin to return it to its naval roots. Navy Strength gins are also now produced by a number of distillers around the world. Four Pillars Gin in Australia offers a Navy Strength gin, as does Far North Spirits in Minnesota, USA. Hayman's Royal Dock Gin is another British Navy Strength gin.

Old Tom styles of gin have also seen a revival. The Poetic License Distillery in the North East of England produces an Old Tom style of sweetened gin, as does Hernö Gin from Sweden, which uses both meadowsweet as a botanical and a small amount of added sugar to impart the characteristic Old Tom sweetness to this version of their gin. Hayman produces an Old Tom-style gin that incorporates liquorice as a botanical, referencing an original recipe for this style of gin.

Opposite: The Gin Fizz, made with gin, lemon and sugar syrup shaken with ice. The repertoire of today's cocktail makers and mixologists continues to grow with ever more inventive ways of consuming gin. (Will Shenton/CC3.0)

An advertisement for Tanqueray No. Ten from the early twenty-first century. The spirit is one of many premium gins now being produced by large distillers and is named after the still in which it is manufactured. (Diageo)

A Martinez cocktail, originally made using old tom style gin, is widely regarded as a forerunner of the now more famous Martini. (Will Shenton/CC 3.0)

It would be too simplistic to portray the large-scale production of distillers such as Gordon's, Beefeater and Tanqueray as totally distinct from that of the small, craft gin producers. The large producers have also innovated and today produce a range of specialist products. Tanqueray, for example, produces Tanqueray No. Ten in a small pot still first used in the 1930s. With the focus on the many small-scale innovative producers of gin, some of the large and established manufacturers can be overlooked. Beefeater is the only London Dry gin that has been produced in the city since 1876 – quite a heritage. These companies today produce huge quantities of gin: Gordon's accounts for just short of half of all gin sold in the UK with Beefeater the next largest in terms of market share.

The range of gins available today is truly remarkable and far removed from the drink produced in bathtubs and drunk in back alleys in the eighteenth century. Integral to this diversity is the use of innovative and unusual botanicals. While all gin continues to use juniper as its key botanical, the inventiveness of distillers today in searching out new flavours is incredible. One gin, produced by Zymurgorium in Manchester, includes flavours derived from marmalade. Several gins incorporate flavours drawn from tealeaves, including Teasmith Gin, Yorkshire Tea Gin and Adnams Rising Sun Gin.

Fruits are also commonly used in craft gin production today. A modern take on the traditional sloe gin is Mulberry Gin produced by Boodles, which also incorporates flavours of

MARTINEZ

INGREDIENTS

30ml Old Tom gin

60ml sweet vermouth

2 dashes of maraschino liqueur

1 dash of Boker's Bitters

A slice of lemon

METHOD
Fill a bar glass half full of ice and add ingredients. Strain into cocktail glass. Add olive or cherry to taste, garnish with lemon peel.

ST. GEORGE

Handcrafted in California

BOTANIVORE

GIN

*Botanical balancing act
Perfect order, pot distilled
balanced juniper and...
honey of choice herbs,...
...ces and citrus*

...EN ALC. BY VOL.

ST. GEORGE

Handcrafted in California

DRY RYE

GIN

*An assertive and elegant
American dry gin to
delight the unabashed
juniper lover*

45 PERCENT ALC BY VOL.

45% ALC. BY VOL.

Lot No. GR2011-03

ST. GEORGE

Handcrafted in California

TERROIR

GIN

*A uniquely Californian gin
with a sense of place and poetry.
Distilled from sustainably
sourced botanicals*

45 PERCENT ALC BY VOL.

45% ALC. BY VOL.

Lot No. GT...

ST. GEORGE

Handcrafted in California

DRY RYE

GIN

*An assertive and elegant
American dry gin to
delight the unabashed
juniper lover*

...% ALC. BY VOL.

The still affectionately known as 'Ugly Betty' at the Bruichladdich Distillery, manufacturers of The Botanist Gin. The still is a Lomond Still, an innovative still developed in Scotland in the 1950s. (Image courtesy of Bruichladdich Distillery)

raspberries and currants. Brockmans Gin is infused with blackberries and blueberries. Caorunn uses wild rowan berries as a botanical. There are also some remarkable gins produced in America today: Greenhook Ginsmiths American Dry Gin is produced using techniques more readily associated with French *parfumerie* techniques. And a new take on the worm found in some makes of tequila is Anty Gin, which is infused with 62 wood ants per bottle.

One of the most significant features of the range of gins produced today is the strong sense of place created by the use of local, regional botanicals, for example, St George Spirits,

The range of gins produced by St George Spirits. Botanivore uses nineteen different botanicals to give a spirit with real depth of flavour and character. (St George)

California. By using local botanicals including Douglas fir, California bay laurel and coastal sage, the distillers capture the essence of the region in which the gin is manufactured. One of the St George gins, the intriguingly named Botanivore, uses nineteen different botanicals in total.

Bruichladdich Distillery goes even further, using twenty-two locally foraged, wild botanicals from the island of Islay in addition to nine classic botanicals to give as much local flavour to their gin as is present in the whisky which the island is so noted for. These include gorse, bog myrtle and downy birch as well as a small amount of Islay juniper. A full-time forager gathers these local botanicals from around the island. Another example of an island distillery incorporating local flavours is the Isle of Harris Gin, which uses sugar kelp as one of its botanicals.

One of the principal differences between gin and whisky (a key reason it has often attracted bootleggers, whether in eighteenth-century London or twentieth-century Chicago) is that it does not need to be matured. This does not mean, however, that ageing cannot be used to impart flavour to gin, and it is something a number of distillers are working on in the twenty-first century. Beefeater produces Burrough's Reserve, an oak-aged gin named after the company's first master distiller. Hayman's cask-rested gin sees the spirit rested in whisky casks for three weeks to help draw out the flavour of the spirit.

Opposite: The master forager James Donaldson, responsible for obtaining the Islay botanicals used in The Botanist Gin. The botanicals used to flavour the gin are contained in the bag seen here, described as resembling a giant tea bag. (Image courtesy of Bruichladdich Distillery)

De keuze uit :

* GBK Moutwijn Jenever.

* Roosenwater Kruiden Likeur

* De kuyper Anisette.
  Samen € 1.⁵⁰

This chapter brings the history of gin up to date. Having evolved from its early roots in medicinal tonics and the Low Countries' jenever, the spirit caused a moral panic in the eighteenth century, took advantage of new technology in the nineteenth, and then its popularity rose, dipped and rose again the twentieth and twenty-first centuries. Today the gin drinker can enjoy an incredibly diverse range of high-quality spirits, which can only bode well for the future of this intriguing, enigmatic drink.

iStock

FURTHER READING

This list includes just some of the many fascinating books to expand the enthusiast's knowledge of gin beyond what is contained here.

BOOKS

Coates G. *Classic Gin*. Prion, 2000.

Craddock, H. *The Savoy Cocktail Book*. Girard and Stewart, 2015 (reprint of 1954 original).

Dillon, P. *The Much-Lamented Death of Madame Geneva*. Thistle Publishing, 2013.

Haigh, T. *Vintage Spirits and Forgotten Cocktails*. Quarry Books, 2009.

Solmonson, L.J. *Gin: A Global History*. Reaktion Books, 2012.

Thomas, J. *How to Mix Drinks*. Hesperus Press Ltd, 2009.

Williams, O. *Gin Glorious Gin*. Headline, 2015.

WEBSITES

Difford's Guide: www.diffordsguide.com

Gin Foundry: www.ginfoundry.com

Cocktail recipes: www.liquor.com

PLACES TO VISIT

JENEVER

For those who wish to trace the origins of gin through jenever, there are several places of interest to visit in the Low Countries:

National Jenever Museum, Lange Haven 74–76, 3111 CH
   Schiedam, Netherlands. Telephone: 031 (0)102469676.
   Website: www.jenevermuseum.nl
Jenever Museum, Witte Nonnenstraat 19, 3500
   Hasselt, Belgium. Telephone: 032 (0)11239860.
   Website: www.jenevermuseum.be
House of Bols, Paulus Potterstraat 12, 1071 CZ Amsterdam,
   Netherlands. Telephone: 031 (0)205708575.
   Website: www.bols.com

LARGE PRODUCERS

Visitor centres and distillery tours:

Beefeater Gin, 20 Montford Place, London SE11 5DE.
   Telephone: 020 7587 0034.
   Website: www.beefeaterdistillery.com
Black Friars Distillery, 60 Southside Street, The Barbican,
   Plymouth PL1 2LQ. Telephone: 01752 665292.
   Website: www.plymouthdistillery.com

Bombay Sapphire Distillery, Laverstoke Mill, Whitchurch, Hampshire RG28 7NR. Telephone: 01256 890090. Website: www.distillery.bombaysapphire.com

Adnams, Pinkney's Lane, Southwold, Suffolk IP18 6EW. Telephone: 01502 727225. Website: adnams.co.uk

CRAFT PRODUCERS

There are now many that can be visited:

Edinburgh Gin Distillery, 1a Rutland Place, Edinburgh EH1 2AD. Telephone: 0131 656 2810. Website: www.edinburghgin.com

Cotswolds Distillery, Phillip's Field, Whichford Road, Stourton, Shipston-on-Stour CV36 5HG. Telephone: 01608 238533. Website: www.cotswoldsdistillery.com

Sipsmith, 83 Cranbrook Rd, Chiswick, London W4 2LJ. Telephone: 020 8747 0753. Website: www.sipsmith.com

Penderyn Distillery, Penderyn, Rhondda Cynon Taf CF44 0SX. Telephone: 01685 810650. Website: www.penderyn.wales

Manchester Three Rivers Gin, City of Manchester Distillery, 21 Red Bank Parade, Manchester M4 4HF. Telephone: 0161 839 2667. Website: www.manchesterthreerivers.com

Echlinville Distillery, 62 Gransha Rd, Newtownards
    BT22 1AJ. Telephone: 02842 738597.
    Website: www.echlinville.com
City of London Distillery, 22–24 Bride Lane, London
    EC4Y 8DT. Telephone: 020 7936 3636.
    Website: www.cityoflondondistillery.com
Bruichladdich Distillery, A847, Bruichladdich, Isle of Islay
    PA49 7UN. Telephone: 01496 850190.
    Website: www.bruichladdich.com
Chase Distillery, Chase Farm, Rosemaund Drive, Preston
    Wynne, Hereford HR1 3PG. Telephone: 01432 820455.
    Website: www.chasedistillery.co.uk
East London Liquor Company, GF1, 221 Grove Rd, London
    E3 5SN. Telephone: 020 3011 0980.
    Website: www.eastlondonliquorcompany.com

GIN PALACES
Experience something of the Victorian gin palace:

The Princess Louise, Holborn, London
Princess Victoria in Uxbridge, London
The Philharmonic Dining Rooms, Liverpool
Bakers Vaults, Stockport
The Bartons Arms, Birmingham
Crown Liquor Saloon, Belfast
Guildford Arms, Edinburgh

INDEX